EVENTUALITIES

By John Birtwhistle

POETRY

The Conversion to Oil of the Lots Road London
Transport
Power Station, and Other Poems

Vision of Wat Tyler

Haysaving: a Connemara Journal

Tidal Models

Our Worst Suspicions

A Selection of Poems

LIBRETTI

The Plumber's Gift. Opera in Two Acts

The Griffin's Tale. Legend for Baritone and Orchestra

The Fabulous Adventures of Alexander the Great

Rings of Jade. Poems from the Prison Diaries
of Ho Chi Minh

John Birtwhistle

Eventualities

ANVIL PRESS POETRY

Published in 2013
by Anvil Press Poetry Ltd
Neptune House 70 Royal Hill London SE10 8RF
www.anvilpresspoetry.com

This book is published with financial assistance
from Arts Council England

Designed and set in Monotype Ehrhardt by Anvil
Printed and bound in Great Britain
by Hobbs the Printers Ltd

ISBN 978 0 85646 451 5

A catalogue record for this book
is available from the British Library

for Mireille
with an amber pendant

Futile to resist, O
succulent Fly,
such sticky resin. We die
into stone for an artist
of species unborn,
adorning a woman
needless to adorn.

CONTENTS

Eventualities

A 'CADAVER TOMB'

A winded mole on his back, his legs to the four winds
his belly an erupting crater of maggots

On our last walk together before you left home
you were just as curious about this exploded diagram

as once you were touched by the creature waving
soft spades from his hill in your favourite toy

On a child-level shelf below the marble corpse
of a dignified bishop lies his monstrance of leather

writhing with wildlife as though a maggoty dance
and minute cycles of rot were his chance of new life

Look, children. Who can spot the snail, the mouse,
the beetle, the lizard, the frog and the littler worms?

Leaving the passers-by to reflect on what passes
and what we are passing through, and pity old Bishop Mole

A LITTLE GIRL ASLEEP

her clear forehead   her crescent eyes
formal as the tiny Hepworth

she carved with her finger nail
into a white oval of soap

A PAINTING IS NOT A THING

It may be looted, locked in vault or dining room
but a painting is not a thing and cannot be possessed

It may be aborted, abandoned or destroyed
sold, bequeathed or seized in lieu of tax

but in truth a painting is owned by no one
It will for ever belong to the moment of seeing

by anyone who sees it well. The rest is for auctioneers

A SHADOW LEANS AGAINST A TREE

There's nothing to be thought
I gaze at a broken bubble fixed in the glaze of a mug
He'll be going into theatre just about now
The key to the box is locked inside the box

*

In the beech tree's pool of shade
a few hailstones are not yet melted
Hailstones with dog violets
A thing my friend may never see again

A SPOT OF TIME

—— Be that as it may.
The summer also held a livelier theme
And germ of brighter thought. Unlikely source
Though school exams will be for youth's delight,
It was a text – of all things, a Set Book –
That put me to the study of my heart.

It was the year that Kennedy was shot
And other scenes, uncannily, were stopped
In their procession to forgetfulness
And burned into our memories of where
That news was shown. So, in a flashbulb, I
Can forcibly recall the very fence –
The traffic din beyond, the quiet here;
The standard oak or gnomon of the day
Whose patchy sunlight, sunlight-mended shade,
Would cross our lawn; likewise the kitchen chair
I shifted through the hours as I read
The Prelude and its power was set in train,

For then it came upon me in a flash:
This verse of language, this is wonder-full.

ALBA

Listening in white dawn
   to the kinds of birds
   and for all the song
that has been made of this

new light flickering through
   slight specks in the weave
   of curtains giving
to our bright coverlet

we know again what is
   about to impinge

Morning tickles the day
   into surfacing
   from its drowned valley
only to bring to light

the down of your shoulder
   green veins in your wrist
   ways you seem to have
trickling into being

with the morning and with
   the fragrance of sound

Seedlings begin again
 The room is opened
 by tints of almond
alive to this moment

frail corals of light
 steadily building
 patches of detail
on the hand on the quilt

Filtering curtains gain
 again their effects

Despite its nervous ways
 light's no animal
 nor looks down on us
with savage moral will

It is in our own eyes
 the white or as yet
 vaguely dark shall find
their eventual form

and the day ask of us
 what we make of it

ALEXANDER TO CHARON

Here is my coin. You will know the face
That sent you cargoes of shades, in my day.

AMONGST HISTORY DONS

On shutting Sisman's biography of Trevor-Roper

Who knows whose reason is the madder
Or can tell the viper from the adder?

ARCHAEOPTERYX

a feral pigeon rolled flat
into the tarmac

AS TO WHETHER BOG-COTTON HAS ANY PRACTICAL USE

for Judy Donovan

That silvery flower
of the Bog-Cotton is chiefly used

For twisting into candlewicks
For stuffing pillows in olden days
For praising by simile
      the shoulders and adjacent parts of maidens
For plucking at emigrant heartstrings
For laying claim
      to our native flowers in the world anthology
For dressing wounds

A gloss

snow is white as white can be
until the cotton flowers
   drift their summer snow

Three encouragements on the road

A plank of sunlight
A pool of cotton
A fairy spring

From lost Gaelic verses in admiration of a callow youth

Your silky hairs are to be desired
And taken between my fingertips

    a tuft of cotton
    fluffs in the breeze

ATTEMPTS AT ALCMAN

Night. Silence of the whole valley.
A line of Alcman active in my mind.

Greek lyric poet, flourished 620 BC. Born in Lydia? Said to have lived as a slave in Sparta where he was granted freedom as reward for his skill. Best known for his fragment on night.

Along the edges of the hills
Horizon trees are delicate as flowers

The houses in their valley sleep
Like mosses in a rocky cleft
And honeybees are quiet in their combs

Yet lines of Alcman's are alert
The feelers of a moth are quivering
Dark nests are watchful in the crowns

Against the edges of the hills
There runs a jagged glare of midnight sun

or:

Against the edges of the hills there runs a gleam
Of midnight sun
The few windows have fallen blind
A bank of deeply saffron flowers have closed their eyes
Cones of daylight clenched around their stems

And so for birds of every kind
And in the eyes of the world there is nothing but rest
   But there is a line
   By a Lydian slave
That weighs upon my mind

    or else:

I praise Alcman for having praised
A tightrope girl for balancing an earthen jar

Of lioness milk along the moonlit air
To make that cheese of a moon

AUDEN COLLEGE IN WINTER

for Colin Edwards

Study these that step across a lake
Lonely leaders of the examined life
Scruffy to public conscience yet
Often clever, sometimes ever so,
    Young men in one another's verse
    Yearning for lost soprano voice.

Revise how mignon tufted duck
Dive like small change at the wish
Of pairs of learners as they merge
In long vacations of the unassessed
    As gulping carp slurp up the sludge
    And greylag geese excogitate the Weird.

And mark: this view is freezing fast,
That coot retires, those geese are slithering,
Whilst milky jets in fits and starts
Chuck polar bear cubs into gelid air
    To fix them as parabolas of ice,
    A frozen fountain of desire.

BEING ASKED BY MY MOTHER
WHICH OF MY FATHER'S THINGS
I SHOULD LIKE TO BE GIVEN

The arrow head. You know –
that ivy flint-leaf he
told us he'd found in his youth
climbing Inkpen Beacon.
Just spotted it. In his path.

It must be somewhere.
A triangle of black flint
you could fit on a ha'penny,
daintily flaked, with tang
and barb nicked into the base.

I think him alone, don't imagine
his 1930's rig
or even his face; I am within
that vigorous day of skylarks
views and unsought finds.

Never mind; I have it already,
my sense of the instant
his anecdote was knapped, shot
and lay to be found. Give me that.
It's that has the barb and tang.

BILDUNGSROMAN

My son is reading *The Catcher in the Rye*
for the first time.
                    Am I sighing to be
his age and reading *The Catcher in the Rye*?

BUILDINGS

and their local nicknames

Observe the iron dinosaur that grabs
window, door and corridor
from the familiar *Wedding Cake*

where Sheffield couples used to make
their keys to turn in everlasting locks,
nestling by the chill *Egg Box*.

Both of those demolished now, we
are the only keepers of our vow.
This new year of our marriage I renew

all the promises I made to you.
Love, let us live attentively before
we too are grappled by the dinosaur.

CONVERSATION

As I walked past a caff in a strange part of town
you tapped on the sweaty pane to beckon me in
I sat down opposite as though an expected friend

The shadowy youth at the counter did not stir
his gaze transfixed by a plastic orange damned
to float around in its drum of watery juice

I asked, How're you keeping?   *Could be worse*
You're a better colour   *Got over the jaundice*
How are they treating you?   *Not bad, considering*

Get anything off for your service?   *Not a day.*
Same as the pension fund. You pay all your life
and it's nothing but snowflakes settling on water

Not lost your turn of phrase then   *That I did*
give you   You always told me the cost of your gifts
(and in this silent conversation, I silently weep)

When all's said and done, I taught you to speak
and read and write with stories night after night
'and my profit on't is I know how to curse'

I even gave you 'red plague' with my flash
of Trotsky   You watched me take down that book
but never came clean what ever it meant to you

Too late now   Apparently not   *(Silence)*
I was too harsh   Now you tell me   *(Silence*
The same sterile fruit going round and around)

How long has it been? *A whole generation.*
And now you're a father yourself Yes, despite
the 'sins of the fathers' you used to preach

It took me a while to work out what that meant
It took me a while too, by the way. Every so
often I catch myself echoing your words

or tones of voice, or carrying out some action
of yours. The crumbs on this table, for instance:
you'd've brushed them with the edge of your palm

off the tabletop to the cup of your other hand.
From that you'd give them to sparrows, thus!
Just look at those sparrows, squabbling in dust

I have to be going, there's a hole I have to dig.
I think   we   should   forgive   each   other.
There are things that go without words

No, don't weasel me, it's far too late for that.
How you were, was part of a history shared –
which is the only sense I can give to 'forgive'

There are certain things that go without saying
Speak those uncertain things, or how can I know
you feel, for your part, there's ought to regret

or whether I am forgiven also? A word would...
When all's said and done (which it is, by the way...)
Brimming with silence, he had almost said...

when the youth sauntered over and presented our bill.
Few meaty remarks; no drink; unspokens on the side.
It came to so many snowflakes settling on water.

CYPRESS: AN ODE

The shrine is encircled by tall cypress trees
And out of that soil a profusion of springs
Flow silently. There, Apollo stoops to bathe

And there a sapling grows that once was a youth,
Cypress by name. It is the beauty of the tree
That makes the transformation plausible.

— PHILOSTRATUS, *Life of Apollonius*

Here is no shrine to transformation; even waterfalls
Fall silently; enchanted glades
Are no defence of verse where pilgrims quest
For changeless verities.
Yet we travel to disclose our homeless thoughts
Where cypress trees are silhouettes of flame
That scorch the underlying streams to flow unsplashingly.

As for the youth so casually calm, unshouldering
His backpack, encompassed by trees
Of exalting height, breathing unbreathed air
In the spring of his day,
Already a portion of that which merely
Being young entitles him to, he stuffs
A plastic bottle into the cleft of a tree, and pees.

A second celebrant, or nymph of this place, comes bearing
Vegetarian sacrifice
In a floral basket of her own weft.
A third is plucking at
A homemade pentatonic lyre. None the less
A sapling thrill arises from this ground,
And shades that nurture our wish for flamelike changes
      of form.

In the eye of cold philosophy, a tree will take shape
After its own repeating style
Written in almost immutable code
Forever conifer;
The comely God Himself, descending to bathe
Was merely a fanciful way to see
Nothing more than reflected sun as it sets in a pool

Just here, the very place where it is said that He implored
Sad Cypress to set himself free
From an inordinate grief, having killed
The creature he most loved;
But Cypress was growing already within
His own body that sweeping bronze-dark tree
He was soon to become, arrested in its weeping spire,

For did he not unbend from his trunk the bristling limbs,
Splintering his skin to unfold
His cancer or his travesty of birth
In changing loveliness,
Stabbing, splitting his grieving self inside out,
Then to absorb his needles from the floor
As he expressed himself as an emblem for any grief?

Although the deeply enfolding shade goes on lording it
Over us, subduing our thought,
We begin to notice a few ripples
In this black-green water,
The lyre retreating before the weir's chuckle,
And teasing reflected glimpses of sky
That we'd never have seen in inwardly reflective trees;

So we're able to take our leave of that enchanting place
And drive away through verticals
– A cypress grove by gloomy yard of graves –
Transected by distant
Diagonals of white turbine blades fringing
Bright plains of mechanized sunflower fields,
Thinking from time to time of Cypress, his beautiful tree.

ELOISE AMONGST THE PIGEONS

A toddler makes to chase pigeons

They commote, they glide back to her
Only to be flustered again into wheeling

Back to her voice. She returns, out of
Breath: 'I want to see . . . I want to see

'Everything, in the WHOLE WORLD'

ETHNIC MONITORING

The well-meaning form demands
my tick in a single
                    box for your race
so many fields compressed in a bud.

You went searching through the vaults
of a vast library
                    to borrow your sequence
some of it latent for hundreds of years.

Who cares if these are your father's eyes?
or your Viking hair
                    a raid on Lincolnshire
or a white African settler's trait?

Did the Mongol invasion of Norway
give rise to your
                    epicanthic folds?
Are these thoughtful fingers

those of a Jura watchmaker? Whoever
could have dumped
                    your infant grandpa
on a Leeds doorstep? Vain questions now

we can print out the long involved spirals
of heredity.
            So, familiar stranger
ticked as 'White Other', I gaze along

escapingly subtle curves of your brow,
the bones of your skull
                            continents drifting
together. I exult that you have fetched

your codes from every quarter, and that
so many variables
                        compose your
secret head.   I kiss   your fontanelle.

FIRST SIGN, A SHARP WHITE MOON
AS IF THE CAUSE OF SNOW

first sign, a sharp white moon
as if the cause of snow

Michael Finnissy took this as the title for his composition *First
Sign, A Sharp White Moon As If The Cause Of Snow* for piano +14
(1968), revised for solo alto flute (1975) as *First Sign, A Sharp
White Moon As If The Cause Of Snow*.

FORMS OF MODERNITY

The University of Glasgow advertises a course on Romanticism
and the Forms of Modernity *using William Blake's* Ancient of
Days *overprinted like a supermarket bargain with a five-pointed
star to proclaim that it is* '5 ★ RATED' *by the Government.*

Behold the Forms of Modernity striding the Dark Age,
The grand dividers, the instruments of calculation
And division, dividing into ever finer degrees.
The Ratio repeats itself in dull and duller round.

Five stars light the cavern'd Man; five spears tyrannical,
For what was once only imagin'd is now research'd
And the five senses tutor all perception & desire
And Glasgow echoes Publish! Publish! and Be Saved!

HIS WIDOW GAVE ME

a black electric razor
filled with silver dust

HÖLDERLIN IN BORDEAUX

Rain stings my face
I rush along the pavement
Those rivers of trees that flex within the storm
Elegant façades racing by

Their poplars bowing and rebounding before
Willows can recover
In symphony of river and branching trees
And only now bending back to spread
Wide the swim of their boughs

Rational squares revolve
To pulse again in wake and reawakening against
This wind as lesser trees are having their say
Swaying more rapidly to and fro

I tear along these avenues that split the buildings
Down to the Theatre its charade of Muses
Its intolerable colonnade of public men

I jeer as carriages are passing me by
Their tinted windows their fragrant women
Their contemptuous fog of courtesy

Currents rejoining in immense rivers of trees
Dissolving rational squares

A line of poplar trees being a tremendous comb
That sings and soars above that passive mass of trees
That sways and would appear to sing

Monuments bellow to the storm
To sleep is shameful

And I am shouting over the storm
It Is Only Great Music That Matters

HOW IT WAS A CHILD SPOTTED THE HERON

The stream was taking a line of music for a walk

when you froze in our path and hardly dared point
to a heron   quite still   in hunting poise on a stone

Our eyes opened wide at its beak   its tiny eye
     sharply concentric as a scissor screw

bird on stone   you on bank   watching the heron
watching you watch   unblinkingly alive to the stream

IL GRAN RIFIUTO

Has any man been preferred before you at a banquet, or in being honoured or invited to council? Remember that you could not have obtained those things without paying his price.

What is the price of a lettuce? An obol perhaps. If a man lose his obol to gain a lettuce, and you have no lettuce but keep your obol, do not suppose that you receive less than him.

— EPICTETUS, *Enchiridion*

Lost the lettuce but kept my coin
Kept my talent, lost the gain
Lost the mustard but kept my seed
Kept my council, lost the vote
Lost the battle. Kept my fingernail

'IN ENGLAND NOW A-BED'

I concede that my comparison between
the crumpled sheet across a double bed
and the mountains of Afghanistan
was superficial and unworthy of either.

I can see clearly now that a bed sheet
is a single layered, relatively light weight
topologically continuous
soft and flexible fabric, whereas

rocks are many-layered, crushingly
heavy, fractured, sharp and brittle
although their properties may change
and, under unwitnessed pressure, flow.

It follows that those long ridges stretching
between summits like ideal snowy routes
would collapse, the many overhangs
would break under their own weight

and that I must retract my futile simile
made in the frightening light of dawn
which meant no more than to be aghast
at the map they face, their boys and ours.

IN FARGATE

In Fargate, Sheffield, where the Dutch florist
sets out his tablets of colour like a strict
field planted by Mondrian, a Burmese woman

stands entranced at blue waterlily heads
one to a flask, in martial array

I can taste it
  now. Mother
    used to send us

in a rowing boat
  to gather lily
    roots from the lake

I am leaning
  over the side
    plunging through

flowers to grasp
  the ever so sweet
    slippery stuff

We'd chew it before
  it ever got
    to the kitchen fire

Floating like lilies my sister and me

IN THE MIDST OF THE CITY
WE ARE IN WOODS

for Allen Capes

The mist this morning has a sniff of surrounding woods
of leaf mould and smouldering leaves wafted here
from hills where the autumn woods are.

In a second-hand bookshop a man unwraps
woody brown mushrooms from a must of newsprint
'Too early this year,' he is telling me, 'Like everything is.'

IN THE PUBLIC GARDENS, BORDEAUX

for Josephine and Marc Dubreuil

Geh aber nun und grüße
Die schöne Garonne,
Und die Gärten von Bordeaux

— FRIEDRICH HÖLDERLIN, *Andenken*

Gilded gates make a sprightly
entrance to one of those spaces
once noble now democratic, as open
as any we have, a 'field full of folk'

The *petit peuple* have been let in
beggars even, even the demented lady
led about by kindly keepers showing
her to her delight the ring of girls

delightedly linking hands like girls
torn into being by dextrous hands
for an absurd paper chain to mock
surrounding statues' classical pose:

That Arcadian shepherd leaning,
lest he snap at the ankle, against
a goatskin spread on a stump
tootling on his throttled flute

ignores his modern avatar
bearing a bicycle wheel to be trued
yet both gain entrance and those
rectified persons, those of note

in virtue of their stones, assume
a quietly overgrown place amongst
the paths and threatening sprigs
of which Nature used to remind

   Rain upon stone has for so long
revised the youth whose marble
puberty must wrestle forever
with his own Chimera to retrieve

his lyre, broken between her claws
– Oh amorous allegory! –
for a statue cannot take a statue
into its arms as a sculpture may.

Nevertheless the sinuous rivulet
continuously giving back the gaze
upon such flexible dreams
will reflect our mingled thought . . .

   That look so fixed within the trees
of solid worthies resigned onto
their plinths, and those deliberate
buildings, yet afford a certain play

as though formality might not
after all be the only power.
Walkers on terraces perhaps
linger to gaze on playpen dunes

Practical lovers on the bench
can park their pushchair by
an exotic specimen tree
that stands them timely shade

Those infants trapped in a tent
witness all the political science
of puppet theatre and thrill to see
what they could never wish to see

An orator denounces acid rain
to an elderly gent, a puppy
and an Algerian mother dang-
ling a fluffy ball for her child

Slick suits confer by phone
for all the world as though
these public gardens were again
the *bourse de la soirée* of old

That couple back to back
in the bole of a tree may read
one Éluard; the other D'Alembert
Such poles of feeling seem

natural here. The swan regards
the drag of the bank with ripples
of disdain. Then (although the gods
appear no longer to confide in us)

a clump of chestnuts towering
above the roofs just now gave out
an almighty crack. A branch crashed,
stilling the entire space. Nothing spoke.

LINES PINNED TO A STUDY DOOR

When first I read, in cunning Chaucer's line
The lyf so short, the craft so long to lerne
I took the gist for poetry and mine,
The reader's smile so troublesome to earn.

The entrance to your hospital engraves
An ageless maxim of Hippocrates –
ARS LONGA VITA BREVIS – as it braves
The cure for this, our bodies' brief disease.

One phrase distills our art and oath,
A lifelong study for us both.

MAQUIS

Think of the honey from this place
the scent of herbs that fishing boats
know it by, from way out at sea

Think of the honey from this place
and words that lovers take
out of each other's mouths

MAYFLIES

Born in the morning...

an insect leg
        of a jetty straggling into the lake

a coracle
        tied to a stick
                breathing on the shallow swell

... to die at night

MUTED LAMENT

I once heard an absolute of unaccompanied song
in a Connemara kitchen by that proverbial fire
and even then the song was all of long relinquished songs
fallen silent, furled alongside sails of fishing boats

In an English drawing room I clap transcripts
for violin of impressions for voice of a set of folk tunes
and the convivial room applauds a rendering
of our own last echo of long-lost longings of our own

For why should such a formal continuity not be
as moving as the oral stream? The strands of feeling
drawn from her voice evoke our wish to hear the very girl
the violin remembers calling to the fisherman who vanished
out to sea

These lines were written after I heard Robin Ireland play the *Suite Populaire Espagnole*. That work is Paul Kochanski's transcription, from mezzo-soprano to violin, of songs from Manuel de Falla's *Siete Canciones populares Españolas*. Da Falla's songs, composed in Paris in 1914, were themselves modelled on folksongs which had been printed in anthologies – especially, José Inzenga's *Ecos de España* (1874). Such books in turn relied on versions selected and shaped by collectors in the field, who had heard them from singers who knew them by heart.

MY SON FOUND A COW'S PELVIS

As I say, we were out walking and
my son found this gigantic bone
and by hanging it around his neck
it fits him! Archaic breastplate
of a science-fictional Knight.

Walking grew tedious, not least
from bearing of pelvis on chest.
He thought he might hitch a lift.
At this point my experience
came into its own. My dear son,

one thing I do know about is
hitchhiking. Let me tell you,
no one'll ever pick you up on a hill.
And there is no verge to pull onto.
And this is a minor road: no driver

knows where you're thinking to go.
Place yourself at a major junction!
What's more, you're begging strangers
to let you into their car despite
wearing the filthy pelvis of a cow.

At which point a tractor drew up

and took my son I know not where

MY STRIKE-A-LIGHT

*On the Isle of Whithorn on the Solway coast of Galloway
the excavation of graves from the early mediaeval period
turned up a smooth white quartzite pebble about the size of
a hen's egg. Scratches across it show that it had been used
as a 'strike-a-light' for tinder.*

      The pebble had been buried in the grave of a child.

My little light
   My strike-a-light
My spark struck off
   A sharp old age

O bright and likely
   Shining girl
O true, O white
   Most lively stone

Here is stone
   My only lightling
My stricken mite
   So sparky one

NAKED AMBITION HE HAD ALWAYS LOATHED

Preferring that such thoughts of his be clothed.

NUISANCE POETS

After a letter of Seneca

The poet pleads, 'Shall I read
a little more?' 'Oh yes, please do'
praying from our brain of brains
that the bore be struck dumb

After Martial on Ligurinus, who invites one to dinner
just so he can recite from his scroll of verses

Your turbot is exquisite
but we'd prefer your silence

OF THE NATURE OF SATIRE

My newborn son
guzzles half the dug
into his grateful gob

Small hopes from him
of the harsh satirist
his age will require

OFF YOU GO

With how short steps
   arms held out like sugar tongs
      towards me... Very soon

we're on the pavement
   I'm holding your shoulders
      and steadying a bike

After a few goes you can go
   by yourself with my pressing
      hand across your back

until that moment comes
   when the flat of my hand
      across your shoulder blades

feels a slight loss of pressure
   a hint of distance and
      momentum is yours

And the bright module
   now self-contained
      soars out into space

its unwieldy booster
   let loose in slow motion
      peeling away into time

ON SAFE RETURN

Shuffling papers, he notices his Will

Hail, Foolscap. Fleer another day.
Eventually, I'll have my way.

ON THE FELL

Winds have
so cut it it
can give
an edge
to wind

a sand
stone
boulder
sandblasted

to a blade   a breathless bone
releasing these   sharp grains   of sand

OUT OF POMPEII

We call a site a brothel
if it has masonry beds
erotic art and graffiti
    but what about this?

AFRICANVS MORITVR
SCRIBET PVER RVSTICVS
CONDISCES QVI DOLET
    PRO AFRICANO

Africanus is dying
A country boy writes
You can tell who grieves
    for his African

PREPARING HERBS

The pestle speaks:

The mortar speaks:

What is this mood
crashed by smell
a sense not of loss
nor yet released
crushing itself
so as to flavour
my senses now?

You forget
the ground
of our farm
the grounds
of argument
ground and
ground down

REPLY

after Franco Fortini

And now you write to me out of the blue
To say the air in your town on the hill
Is so dry and cool, even as the year
Draws in, that it seems a place to live
Into old age, the climate and the aches
Held in check by thick stone walls.

What prompts you? Who are you, these days?
Perhaps all you needed to be told
Is that you live on in your reedy laugh
Or by some other quirk in the weave.
Why send me word that a dry geranium
Stalk is scratching at your sill?

We had set out, you and I, with slight idea
Of which truths the wind would ask of us –
Or that the countless quarriers
Built in to those safe walls of yours,
And so much work of trees gone into them,
Would one day come to us for the reason.

How free the space then seemed! How strange
The paths over the bald hills into the wind
That had so little to drive against.
We saw the world in our own image
And our parents as unfaithful to us and
Them – of all people! – bodiless and alone.

Because of this the world has turned away
Its face, and we could not be perfect
Or even precise. And yet you laugh
And I can see you distantly in the disc
Down there in the well of our century
That has drawn down so many of our kind.

And so I walk with you among the dead,
Forebears in us of restlessness and words.
And I call you friend amongst the living,
And from how much experience. It was this,
I tell myself, that those ferocious winds
Were about, as they tormented the gardens.

RICE IS A GIVEN

an elegant cone
   against the bitter sun

an elderly man
   at back-breaking toil

'Plant rice
   and harvest slaves'

For rice is a given

   forget the leeches
the golden-apple snails

a snail's silvery traces
   dried out in the sun

For lovely things are tedious

a poet planting ideas
   in delicate lines

Dark seedlings of rice

SEATED FIGURE OF AN OLD LADY

after Celia Paul's paintings of her mother

So still, your frailty becomes a monument.
It is as though I already mourn whom I protect
By drawing this thin curtain to sift the light for you,
Still in the window where you would write to friends.

The room is open at the page 'Help thou mine unbelief'.
You are sitting for the light that veils as it clarifies
And finds by variation all the riches of a single theme,
The artist mother bringing figure from ground.

Wreathed in the thought of children's faithlessness,
You can hear from the yard that the blackbird sings.

SIR ISAAC NEWTON'S CAT

Sir Isaac Newton's cat
Strolling into his study[1] and jumping up[2] onto Sir's lap
Can scarcely be expected to have known[3] that
It had just[4] been the first cat ever to have flapped through a
    cat flap[5]

1.   To reach for a scholarly text
     would only disturb the @
        curled on my lap, into an &
     Therefore I type
       Reference not to hand

2.   Piety, Cognition here co-inhere
     (Slight leavings for the lion's share)

3.   Schrödinger's cat
     Not knowing where it's at
     Is not so very far
     From Erwin Rudolf Josef Alexander Schrödinger trying to
       remember wherever
     the hell it might more probably be that he had parked that diabolical
       device, his car

4.   I enter the kitchen wearing
     specs and a ring. The cat
     stares at me and I tetch at her:
       What's up with you?
       Have you never seen
       a naked man before?

5.   I regret having perpetrated this factoid, which can be traced no earlier than a century after Newton's death. So far as I can discover, the earliest source for the claim is J. M. F. Wright, *Alma Mater; or, Seven Years at the University of Cambridge. By a Trinity Man* (London: Black, Young, and Young, 1827), Vol. 1, pages 17–18. Its influential elaboration by a Church of Scotland minister with a popular readership in America, Andrew K. H. Boyd, in *The Commonplace Philosopher in Town and Country* (London: Parker, Son & Bourn, 1862), page 47, is merely a complacent attempt to bring Newton down to earth. For instance, even if it were true, would it not betoken wit rather than naïvety on Newton's part had he arranged for two holes to be cut in his door, one for the cat and one for its kitten?

SKETCH OF A YOUNG MUSICIAN, INTENT

for Leo

The line of your chin along the rest
reflects the body of the instrument

but not exactly, so as to hint
a tension crouching over the score

A grit in the charcoal catches
lips in fleeting subvocal twitch

Beneath the breathing of the strings
you concentrate and count

SLOWING DOWN TO TURN

                              onto the motorway
              at a wedge of no man's land

we always look out for the gypsy piebald
an edge of ragwort by the field of wheat
with its rope and this morning a foal

SONG

for David Blake

Year after year a swallow tries to nest
on the self-same balcony

Year after year the housewife clears it out
only to find that speck of lime

How can the swallow remember a time
when it was not unwelcome

on that balcony facing south
where year after year it still tries to nest?

SPATE

The clear brook that used to trickle through the woods
conversing with its own valley
is now in full dark peaty spate
throwing aside whatever it will not bear along

its current sucking the ground from under fast boulders
and hard-rooted trees
breaking out and filling fresh parallels as it cuts itself
into a deeper bed

so that in justice to my heart-wounded daughter
and the forces rushing through her
      fiercely crying herself to sleep
I cannot say be at peace

THE MUSEUM OF HICCUPS

an improvisation with a child
to distract her from
an attack of The Hiccups

In the Museum Of Hic
cups there is a collec
tion of famous hic
cups which inc

ludes a plinth for
the loudest ever hic
cup. There's a hic
cup made in sch

ool assembly and a sec
tion by animals
such as cr-ows. In fa
ct there are hic

cups of every desc
ription slow or quick
and for each kind of hic
cup there is a work

sheet for little ki
ds. There are plaques
to say what's in the gla
ss cases and a cle

ver man who hic hic
cupped all his life,
with a small selec
tion of his hiccups

There is a c-ase full
of the best trick
s thought to cure the hic
cup, such as a cup

of clear water, and as
you leave there's a
man with a white stick
hiccupping tunes

THE POET EXPLAINS HIS RELUCTANCE
TO DISCARD A SO-CALLED
CHILDREN'S BOOK

A frog's eye socket   has no floor
so that the eyes   bulge into the mouth
and can be used   to help push food
into the gullet —— No, nor did I.

THE VISIONARY LEAP

That haunt of suicides the Avon Gorge,
Devouring chasm, cliff opposing cliff –
Its woods lamenting Thomas Chatterton
And Thomas Beddoes' poisoned arrow tip –

That gloomy fissure in the upland field,
A savage tear in Bristol's genteel map,
Is measured now and gracefully surpassed.
The sphinx that lurked in its canal is solved.

Brunel! The swoop of your prediction spans
The ancient gap, levels the deep offence.
The forms of your design suspend the laws
Of gravity just as they hold our breath.

Yet this is Nature understood, set forth
Not overcome. The curve catenary
Transmits the secret strength from edge to edge
In harmony with Her unbroken thought:

How far below, the sullen stream that once
Incised this dreadful rift! A remnant now,
It writes its trickle into tidal mud
As though a poet in a far meandering...

TO LIVE BY THE BARRACKS

is to live beside monks
going about their secret ministry

        2

are those camouflage leaves
in slashed cloth
not a version of pastoral?

        3

From their side all the mortar looks in order
From ours it sloshes
as though from the layers of a failed cake

and we grow climbers against our berlin wall

        4

that extensive square
is now a car park for the invalided-out

with a rail for officers to rein their horse

5

on Open Day

a little boy within the armour plate
fiddles with the joystick of

a Rapier ground-to-air missile launcher
and finds the optic quite easy to unscrew

6

tanks always 'roll'
            across the plains
                        into other nations
                                    and through their sullen streets

until this machine starts up with a clank
groan and shrill gnashing of gears

· 7

Today we have daubing of vans
Start at top left with a black blob
Then a sausage of murky green
Proceed to alternate these forms
Until bottom right is attained

whilst on the stray of common land
an entire friesian herd
huddled black-and-white under hawthorn shade
            disruptively presents
a target all but invisible

8

totally deaf
since that explosion in Cyprus
we greet by thumbs-up

9

Once a soldier always a soldier
First a prisoner then a soldier
Then a prison officer

he had thick lenses that magnified his eyes

I suppose you were kindly as you could be?

Oh no, he said, we broke sticks
across their heads

and tears broke into his enormous eyes

10

in this cloister
where unknowns are planned
they
are planting out a fan of bulbs

11

At the gate of castellated brick
with its black arrow slits
and amber level of alert
   a tramp shambles up
   asking for the nearest caff

A sentry with an iron-sighted
L85A2 automatic assault rifle
poking from his shoulder
   brews the old chap
   a lovely cup of tea

   12

           set back from the road
           amidst mature trees
           an unmarked house
           with high blank gates
           closed by keypad

   13

the immortal blackbird struts along the shed
uttering her alarm
because a helicopter is screaming to land

14

and nearby roads called Stables
                        Love Lane
                        Hospital Fields

15

of an evening
a red light at the tip of a radio mast

the sacred heart of Mars

UNSCHEDULED

Short of the capital, our plane
is landed at an airport in deep freeze.
We're kept on board as a line of trucks
take all our baggage from the hold.
Nothing of note but remote snow
ploughs ploughing back and forth
throwing up grey plumes of snow

The trucks return, each suitcase
having been crowbarred open.
The wieldy machine is revolved
and slowly takes off in a low path
across a field of snow on which
a message is trampled in Cyrillic:
O my pilot come back to me AMANDA

VIEWFINDER

Startled by how they ripen one by one,
dangling there as various beads of green
through sunset reds into the full muscat,
I choose a bunch of every subtle tinge,
the purest cluster of translucencies,
focus on shadow crescenting each sphere
to form an image neat as memory,
the background blurred, the trellis out of shot –
but is it for me to be selling wine?

Rather, let one's eye be caught by that wasp
as it seeks a flaw, snips into the skin
and labours to hollow out a vintage,
and so accept the ragged stalk, scuffed bloom,
where someone reached to taste as she prepared
a dinner along the table beneath
for friends to converse over muscatel
and children, running about late, to watch
the stars peep through a canopy of vines.

WAITING AT THE LIGHTS

i.m. George Melly

Those driven by their cars are brought to a halt
Those on the kerb eye up
the figures opposite. Nobody I know

one body I like, and one involved
in daydreams like a day lily
in a traffic of dreams. It is the turn

of our minds to idle in power
a disturbing moment of balance
where purpose hangs, a money

spider on its thread. There is iridescence
in the petrol film on a puddle of rain
and a child cries out: Look Look

Everybody, at the funny Peacock!

WEDDING SONG

to Pam Marshall and Nick Hurst
with a pair of 'Bird of Paradise' flowers

True Birds of Paradise
Never alight or nest
But wing unflaggingly
Throughout the vacant skies
Touching no stone or tree.

If so, let us be false
And take our colours from
Flowers that make their show
In a bird's likeness but
Strike harder roots below.

Grounded, let us delight
In all that draws a stem
From soil of actual things.
Admire the petal's beak.
Observe the annual rings.

WINTER WALK

i.m. Jacques Berthoud

Making our way along the thin scarf of mist
that clings to river thorns, a farther line of trees
a grey comb knotted now and then by nest or mistletoe
or some such canker, the only colour being
iron of dock leaves and rusty wire, he pointed out

a group of farm buildings, outbuildings
and an old wall rounding that previous way of life
and told me that he was minded, come the spring,
to return and make a water-colour study of that
pleasing cluster of forms, were it not for certain

bleeds of iron that could make all this tenuous
as a wisp of spent fireweed adrift in failing light.

The dead have no landscape, tense or mood. How can
the phrase 'The dead' refer? For there is no 'They'.
Their being in the Past is logical, but even so their nouns

betray us with a sense of continuity that cannot hold.
He or his name is but an empty sign. It evaporates
from that which it would signify, nor is there any over-
reigning name to save us from renouncing words
for beings that we know unreal; unlike the present mist

unloosening from other matters this bank of thorns
where he could sparkle in talk of suchlike paradox
and where, as I hold in mind as evergreen, my friend
took notice of skeleton leaves, tincture of rusting share,
the composition of that farm and its retaining line of trees.

YOU GET THE DRIFT

Throughout the wrack of pencils, clips
laps of paper, flotsam from a waterline
strewn across my desk are lips of empty (

) shells once found on those undated
inundated ~~shores~~ by which I keep
the drift / for which I must release the drift

The Griffin's Tale

THE GRIFFIN'S TALE

Legend for Baritone and Orchestra

for Ian Michael

The Griffin is a rare example of a flying quadruped. It is easily recognised by its lion's body and its eagle's head, wings and talons. A Griffin's capacity for air freight is as large as its ferocity. Marco Polo tells of a griffin that broke up an elephant by dropping it out of the sky.

The word Griffin came into English through a fourteenth-century poem about King Alisaunder, known to us as Alexander the Great. This Alexander was a fabulous being, said to have lived in the fourth century of our era and to have conquered the whole of the world then known to the Greeks.

Alexander's legend began with his taming of a famously unmanageable horse. He noticed that the animal was alarmed by its own shadow so that, by facing it into the sun, he was able to calm and mount it. Learning thereby how simple it might be to subdue the world, Alexander set about uniting it by force of arms under Hellenistic ideals. These were to be instilled by a system of gyms and other facilities in a dozen cities all named Alexandria, where he demanded the kow-tow of prostration and kissing the ground – gestures properly due to a god.

Nonetheless, there was a reflective side to Alexander's nature. He interrogated any local sages that fell captive to him, and pestered oracles wherever he went. Visiting Diogenes, he enquired whether there was anything he might bestow on that barrel-dwelling philosopher. 'Yes,' replied Diogenes: 'you can stand out of my light.' The conqueror remarked: 'Were I not Alexander, I would be Diogenes.'

Another of Alexander's fantasies was aerial reconnaissance. He built ladders and hills with which to survey battlefields, as well as venturing on a celestial journey powered by one or more griffins or great carrion birds. The following witness has been collated from the most reliable sources amongst scores of mediaeval romances.

THE GRIFFIN'S TALE

GRIFFIN:

It was a dismal summer, all green and quiet.
We hovered by crossroads, hoping for carrion
      And squawked and squabbled over the helpings.

But then one day the pickings were good. Herds of brutes
On horses clashed and bellowed as they slashed their skins.
      A rosy glut of guts was unhidden.

Peace fell. Such thew and sinew. Such spicy giblets.
And blood as thick as dung. No time to fight – no time
      To wipe your beak. That hour was our finest.

Feasting lulled me. I was resting my head in a
Ribcage when some ruffian clambered on my back.
      It took three or four hops to eject him.

I sank my talons into another fetlock,
But more of these featherless bipeds flung out a net.
      I fought! Lopping and chopping about me.

Useless. They wrapped me in ropes. Then their beast-
                         in-charge
Came to inspect, his rabble bowing and blowing
      Kisses from their claws. Here's what he boasted:

ALEXANDER:

The sky is leaning down
    To meet the earth. The sky
Unrolls its bolt of cloth for me to step upon.
    I am the one to whom it falls
To quell rumour and survey the field.

Just as I bridled the wild horse
    Maddened by its own shadow
By forcing him to face the sun, so now
    I steer my own gaze to the heavens
And defy the oracles.

My historians will echo:

    'It was then that years of research
Into bubbles and rockets
    And scaffolds and special hills
Delivered their terrible seed.'

                    Therefore:

        All these entrails –
            Interpret them.
        Make farthest sightings.
            Predict conquest.

        Abandon work
            On Hills of Surveillance
        Take ironmasters
            From the Star Staircase

And carpenters from
        The Towers of Foresight.
Abort the artificial wings.
        This project has priority.

Let a carriage be built!
        Mount spears at the corners
And a harness on top
        To be drawn by that creature.

His are the wings to haul
        My ship of the air.
Let the hull be strong.
        Make a porthole for me.

For it is my will to see
        As the eagle sees
When he sizes up terrain
        So as to seize his prey.

GRIFFIN:

Well! They kept me awake with their saws'n'their
                                hammers,
Drills and chisels, and they kept me starved. Otherwise,
        I was well treated. Sir, the guards called me.

Then at dawn they breathed on bits of wood, made them
                                glow
And – listen to this – stuck four sweet suckling piglets
        Onto spears and teased them with fire

And sizzled and scorched them under my nostrils,
Turning the dripping grease in the dangles of smoke
    That bore the squealing smells to my senses.

Then, they chained me to that botch of a chariot
And their overlord came back and all saluted
    Him with one raucous voice:

                                        A— le— xan— der!

Next, this Alex loaded himself in the cockpit
And fastened his belt, and I could sniff them fixing
    Those key-babs to the roof at each corner.

The stink was delicious. A hot splutter of fat
Splashed on me pecker. I could stand it no longer.
    Famished, I lurched the job off its moorings.

In ravenous craving I launched it spinning in-
to the sky, twisting around the winds of the co-
    lours of space in a lust for those piglets.

I hoisted higher, but no nearer them skewers.
Ice formed. My quills prickled. Alex was shivering.
    The earth looked like a deep-frozen eyeball.

Hailstones flashed past me. Reeking above me
The meat was still crackling – and as for the cargo,
    I could hear His Nibs muttering prayers:

ALEXANDER:

Nothing, nothing like I thought
  The black air meeting the starry poles
The whole world, as never before

  Spinning in a dark immensity
Our tiny world of time...

How distant my armies
  My splendid horse
How vain the cities bearing my name

  How trivial
My athletes, my engineers

The whole world and its islands
  Passing under my view
A walled town with civil gates

  Fringed with terraces and herds
Meeting utter wilderness

An oasis with its palms and fish
  Receiving trade in wine
Resin, salt, copper and slaves

  From far away across the sand
Beyond any map or hint of good rule

And I laugh to see
How vastly small
Are the accounts of men

Their courtship, strut and pout
Their petty quarrelling

For the liveliness is just as full
In a seedpod snapped
Open by the sun, or

Deep among damp leaves
In the green gulp of a frog

Above all, I can survey
Sea-road and battlefield
Crops, enemy emplacements. Yet

It is the little fly with paper wings
That captures my gaze

And the bulrush by the stream
The tendrils on a vine
The stripy spirals of a snail

And the day of a man
Swift as the hawk's rapture

And always curling around all of this
　　　　The ever-encircling sea
That slowly pulses in its coil

　　　　The world – is a threshing floor
Surrounded by a snake!

But there, there is a river meandering
　　　　For thousands of marches
Through ramparts of mountains

　　　　And there a continent
I could break with a mile of canal

There, a plain of tameable horse
　　　　There, timber for hundreds of ships
There is a precipice, yet at its foot

　　　　The lakeland, the tract of pasture
The vital source of supplies

There is a mountain spurting fire
　　　　There an impassable glacier
There a forest surging with rain

　　　　And there
Is the crucial pass, the way into Persia

GRIFFIN:

At this, a man-like shape with skinny wings and legs
– Nothing to peck at – popped up from behind a cloud
    And (all Greek to me) started announcing:

ANGEL:

Yes, there it lies,
A threshing-floor
Where many flails
Thresh and thrash
To nourish the kingdoms

A threshing floor
Coiled about by its
Blue green snake.
You see it there
Just as you wished.

You pitch your tent
On the field of the world
And it yields to you.
The world is your City:
Alexandria. But

Remember Xerxes
And keep in mind
You are of earthly
Woman born. Raise not
Your head too high.

Now you see it all
And know its boundaries.
Know then your own.
Turn back your spears.
Avoid the gods.

You run the world
You, a glob of spit
That runs about hot iron
And makes a fuss
And, hissing, disappears.

You wear a helmet
You wear a crown
You will be told the truth
By a naked old man
Who lives in a barrel.

GRIFFIN:

So. There I was. Desperate for a slice of pork,
Chained up to a wooden crate in the stratosphere,
    Icicles hanging off of me gnasher,

With some kind of general who was embarking
On a Greek dialogue with an angel. Food for
    Thought's the one thing I just cannot stomach.

So I clawed back the situation. I hurled us
Into a giddy dive, peered in at the pilot's
    Personal porthole'n'gave him a beakful:

Angel-face does have a point, you know. May not have
Much lard on him, but his guts are in the right place.
   Let's get home, eh? Thin air's not for eating.

Think of all the flocks of the world throwing back
Their throats for your fangs. Think of the armies –
   All that flesh gone to waste, such a pity.

Or if innards don't tempt you, think of the kingdoms.
You could have a bit of clout down there, I reckon.
   Let's make a survey; won't take a moment.

But his Highness was still aloft in his raving:

ALEXANDER:

   . . . Now I see it all
And know my place. The narrow

   Sphere of the earth
Must limit my conquest . . .

GRIFFIN:

So I tried on a spot of the old soothsaying:

>Where is the profit in these islands of the sky?
>>You shall gain Persia! Think of the Glory!

That did the trick. He steered down his piglets and crash-
landed, broke the whole box into a pile of planks.
>I flapped away smartish. It made me croak

To watch all his animals rush to devour
Their leader's remains. No more blood, no more feasting
>For that wingless gob called Alexander.

ACKNOWLEDGEMENTS

The cover shows the oil painting *My Mother At Night* by Celia Paul. It is reproduced by kind permission of the artist, her subject and Marlborough Fine Art. I encountered her paintings at her Graves Gallery exhibition, Sheffield, 2005.

'Alba', or 'dawn song', first published by *The Galley Sail Review* (San Francisco) edited by Stanley McNail, is an interlude from *The Plumber's Gift*, an opera composed by David Blake and premiered by English National Opera in 1989. It is reprinted by permission of Novello & Company.

'Auden College in Winter' was first published in *Sphagnum* (York), edited by Colin Edwards.

'Buildings', 'In Fargate' and 'In the Midst of the City. . .' were first published in *The Sheffield Anthology. Poems from the City Imagined* (2012), edited by Ann Sansom and others. 'Buildings' makes play of the local nicknames for the now demolished Registry and head offices of Sheffield City Council.

'Lines Pinned to a Study Door' was presented at a Christmas gathering of the Department of Anaesthesia, Royal Hallamshire Hospital, Sheffield, 2007.

The italics in 'Mayflies' misquote from a lecture on *The Human Interest of Sanskrit Literature* by the Victorian scholar Max Müller.

The recital (2010) mentioned in the note to 'Muted Lament' was held in The Hayshed, Rotherham, through the generosity of Natalie Wing.

'My Strike-A-Light' was published in *BMJ Supportive & Palliative Care*, December 2011, edited by Bill Noble.

'Reply', written with Barbara Garvin, is a version of the late Franco Fortini's poem 'Una Risposta' which, he told us, had been in answer to a letter from his contemporary in Florence, the composer Valentino Bucchi. Together with 'Seated Figure of an Old Lady' and 'In the Public Gardens, Bordeaux', it was first published in the online *Bow-Wow Shop* edited by Michael Glover.

'Song' was written for David Blake's song in the *NMC Songbook* (2008) recording, where it is performed by Jean Rigby (mezzo-soprano) and Huw Watkins (piano). The score, *A Swallow*, is published by University of York Music Press.

A version of *The Griffin's Tale* was also written to be set by David Blake. It was commissioned and premiered by Northern Sinfonia in York, Newcastle and Carlisle in 1995, conducted by Lionel Friend. The baritone Adrian Clarke produced all the voices. Before it was set to music, an early draft of the text was tried out in a rehearsed reading for the Contemporary Opera Studio by the actor John Ramm and (for the rarified voice of the Angel) the counter-tenor Andrew Watts. The initial sources for the piece were drawn from Ian Michael's *Alexander's Flying Machine. The History of a Legend* (University of Southampton, 1974), which I had heard him deliver as an Inaugural Lecture. The score is published by University of York Music Press.

Other debts are implied in dedications and allusions. I am profoundly grateful to all my editors and collaborators.

No factual inference about any person should be drawn from these poems. For instance, my daughter is alive and well and the ghost is not my father.

About the Author

John Birtwhistle was born in 1946. His poetry has been recognized by an Eric Gregory Award, an Arts Council bursary, an Arts Council creative writing fellowship (1976–77, renewed for 1977–78), a writing fellowship at the University of Southampton (1978–80) and a Poetry Book Society Recommendation for *Our Worst Suspicions* (1985). He has had three concert libretti set and performed; of these, David Blake's *The Plumber's Gift* was staged by English National Opera and broadcast on Radio 3. From 1980, he was a Lecturer in English at the University of York before deciding to concentrate on bringing up his children. Since 1992 he has lived in Sheffield with his wife, son and daughter.

Go, my little book
I'd love to come along

As luck would have it
I'm headed another way